CONTENTS

	Acknowledgments	
	Preface	1
1	The Third Eye	3
2	Awakening Your Psychic Power	5
3	Step One – Eat Like a Psychic	9
4	Step Two – Physical Exercise for Psychics	15
5	Step Three – Crystals, Herbs and Essential Oils	19
6	Step Four – Internal Healing	25
7	Step Five – Monitor Your Psychic Progress	31
8	Conclusion	37
	Additional Resources	39

Third Eye Awakening in 5 Easy Steps

Marion Jaide

Copyright © 2014 Marion Jaide

All rights reserved.

No part of this publication may be reproduced in any manner without the written permission of the copyright holder.

Although the author and publisher have made every effort to ensure that the information in this book was correct at release, the author and publisher do not assume and hereby disclaim any liability to any party for any loss, damage, or disruption caused by errors or omissions, whether such errors or omissions result from negligence, accident, or any other cause.

This book is not intended as a substitute for the medical advice of physicians. The reader should regularly consult a physician in matters relating to his/her health and particularly with respect to any symptoms that may require diagnosis or medical attention.

ALSO BY MARION JAIDE

Chakra Healing with Meditation

The EFT Tapping Blueprint

ACKNOWLEDGMENTS

I would like to thank my readers for encouraging me to write this book. I hope you find your psychic powers in due course.

PREFACE

Thank you for purchasing *Third Eye Awakening in 5 Easy Steps!* This book is the ultimate guide to healing the third eye chakra and opening the Pineal gland – where your psychic power is locked.

The Universe contains mysteries and power beyond that we experience in our physical bodies. This *psychic power* allows us to see, feel and hear beyond the physical realm we live in. Such powerful ability is open only to those who seek it and commit themselves to the process of balancing. And if you are seeking this power – you have found the right book.

I have organized this book into 5 steps where we discuss different aspects of the third eye healing including diet, exercise, meditation and monitoring your progress. Healing occurs when we have a balance of physical, emotional and spiritual soothing, so don't skip any steps, and be sure to revisit those you might not focus on every day.

Anyone who seeks psychic power and third eye chakra healing can attain it. By reading and, most importantly, *following through* with the exercises in this book, you can experience and realize your psychic powers too.

1

THE THIRD EYE

What exactly is the mysterious *third eye*?

Our understanding begins with the chakra system: the spinning pools of energy that govern the human body's functioning. Each pool from the Root to the Crown presides over an area of our physical, emotional and spiritual wellbeing. Only once all the chakras are unblocked and free from constriction, can people experience the joy and happiness of an extraordinary life.

The Third Eye chakra according to Hindu scripts is the sixth primary chakra, located at the midpoint of the forehead between the eyebrows, where the pituitary gland is. This chakra is also called the *Ajna* chakra meaning the summoning or command. This chakra energizes our perception and allows us to receive experiences beyond the physical – that is, it is the ultimate gateway to accessing psychic energy. For this reason it's sometimes also referred to as the "Mind's Eye", the "Eye of Horus" or the "All Seeing Eye". Being the sixth of the seven major chakras, it's not a far stretch to imagine where the term *sixth sense* comes from too!

Appropriately, the third eye chakra is also associated with the element of light. Although the third eye doesn't function like the two seeing eyes that perceive the visible spectrum of light, the third eye provides deep vision and works as a channel between conscious and unconscious elements of the mind. It lets people see and receive non-verbal messages from the ether and helps sharpen the senses for improved observation. Denoted by the color indigo – one of the highest frequencies in the electromagnetic spectrum – the third eye is the seat of some of the highest faculties in the human body.

The psychic power the *ajna* chakra grants us is also connected with the seventh or highest chakra called the crown chakra, as this energy pool opens our consciousness to otherworldly experiences. For this reason, opening the third eye chakra for psychic development is synonymous with healing the physical gland associated with the crown chakra, known to us as the *pineal* gland. Moreover, medical research has found the pineal and pituitary glands have been known to pulsate together, like a synchronous unit connecting us with our higher consciousness.

The Pineal Gland

The pineal gland is a small, pine-cone shaped gland, the size of a pea that sits inside your skull near the root of the brain. It is also known as the third eye because this small gland has a lens, cornea and retina just like our physical seeing eyes – so it literally is a third eye!

This gland is physiologically responsible for hormone regulation and the circadian cycle which regulates the body's sleep patterns in response to light. This small gland is responsible for your daily emotions too, as it releases serotonin to make you feel happy and melatonin to generate the feeling of sadness when things aren't so great. However, in the non-physical world, the pineal gland is also the *seat of your soul* and is the physical part of the body in charge of **your psychic power**.

2

AWAKENING YOUR PSYCHIC POWER

While the lower chakras provide sensory inputs from the physical world around us, the open third eye can provide better interpretation of these worldly stimuli. The true undiscovered power of the third eye, however, lies in its ability to grant you access to your innate psychic powers.

Psychic powers have also been known throughout history as *extrasensory perception* - also referred to as *ESP*. You may already know of some psychic powers including levitation and telekinesis (moving physical matter with the mind; however there are many more psychic powers than these. Here are just some of the less known psychic powers said to be granted by an energized, un-constricted third eye:

- **Clairvoyance:** the clear vision to receive otherworldly senses
- **Clairaudience:** the ability to perceive and interpret sound from the ether
- **Astral Projection:** controlling out-of-body experiences through a separate body called the astral body
- **Channelling:** ability to communicate with or through spirits
- **Precognition:** also known as the power of prediction or

the ability to know before things happen

- **Telepathy:** ability to transfer emotions and thoughts in either direction

Perhaps you've come across your own psychic power in life and thought, "that was strange" or "that was great". But they were no coincidences, as you now know, we all have the potential to have open and clear third eyes and access to the psychic gifts we already own.

The Psychic's Health Check

Let's take a look at what a blocked third eye chakra and calcified pineal gland looks like. Read through the following list of constricted third eye chakra symptoms and perform a health check of your psychic powers. Here are some of the other signs or symptoms of a weak third eye chakra:

- Feeling disoriented
- A destructive imagination
- Excessive analysis
- **Frequent headaches or migraines**
- Mood disorders, unhappiness or anger
- Poor memory
- Constant fatigue
- Events causing over stimulation of body and mind
- Oversensitivity to smell, taste and textures
- **Disturbed sleep and nightmares**
- Sinus, nose and chest congestion
- Painful or blurry vision

How did your psychic health check go? If more than 5 of the above resonated with you in some way, you may be suffering from a constricted third eye chakra. But don't feel discouraged if this is you; many people have worked through their symptoms to achieve third eye healing and psychic activation. Just following some of the steps in this book will mean you can heal your third eye too.

Why Is My Third Eye Blocked?

The concept of the third eye has been highly revered all throughout history and ages from the ancient Egyptians, to the Eastern philosophies and is featured on the US one dollar bill. There's even a courtyard and statue dedicated to this pinecone-shaped gland in the Vatican City. It seems regardless of culture, geography or era, there is an interest in the Third Eye.

Although the third eye has been known for so long in history, the primary reason we are unaware of the third eye or our psychic ability is that if not exercised or nurtured, our psychic awareness becomes dormant. This is most commonly realized when the pineal gland becomes calcified (a real, medical term for hardening by a thin coating of calcium phosphate) before we hit puberty.

There are times when we are solely responsible for our own chakra constrictions. We live every day with fears, worries, anxieties about losing our jobs or uncertainty about paying bills. Lack of confidence and poor self-worth are also chakra killers. But other people in our lives may also end up worsening a blockade if they are not supportive, are too demanding or are disturbing our energy fields.

There are also emotional elements to the third eye. Blockages in your *ajna* chakra are caused by illusions developed during your lifetime. These illusions limit your perception of the world and more importantly, your connection with all things and the Universe. Without a balanced third eye chakra, you are unable to look at the big picture objectively. Your time, energy and efforts will remain dedicated to the wrong things.

Regardless of the causes of your third eye constrictions, your third eye healing starts now. The following 5 chapters will describe each of the steps necessary to clear your third eye and open the pineal gland.

Prognosis: Your Third Eye Healing

The third eye chakra is difficult to open, because unlike emotions and physical experience, we don't get instant feedback of progress. Despite this, I encourage all readers to stick to the Third Eye Awakening steps and keep the end goal in mind: tapping into our infinite psychic power.

Third eye awakening is achieved with a balanced combination of external healing methods like yoga, crystals and essential oils in coordination with internal methods like meditation.

To start our third eye awakening we will begin with external methods by examining the proper diet, exercises and alternative therapies to *decalcify* the pineal gland and activate it out of dormancy. These are steps 1 to 3 in our 5 step system. Following this we will continue our third eye awakening through internally focused meditation and monitoring of our psychic powers in steps 4 and 5.

Don't struggle with living a mediocre life full of misconceptions. Heal your third eye chakra and awaken your infinite psychic power to live life on the next level.

3

STEP ONE – EAT LIKE A PSYCHIC

The reason many of our third eye chakras aren't healed is because of obsession and attachment with the physical world. The best way we can remove ourselves from this physical vortex and start to experience the fuller psychic energy within is to eat a natural diet and work on our third eye energy.

Fruits and Vegetables

Most of us have eating habits are harmful for our spiritual growth and slows it down. Food plays a more important role than we thought in keeping our chakras active and healthy. To make it easier for you to choose, we have divided the food articles into two broad categories: **acid-forming** and **alkaline-forming.**

Acid accumulation causes calcification of the pineal gland which is not good for your third eye chakra healing. I know, I know, everyone loves eating chocolate cake, roast dinners and fizzy drinks, but just think how every additional bite of these worldly, calcifying foods is blocking your psychic healing! They're also not great for your waistline too!

You should concentrate on eating more alkaline foods as they enhance your intuition, psychic power, dreams, sense of peace, happiness and creativity. Some alkaline fruits and vegetables have been listed below so you can choose your favourite foods rather than sticking to the same meals which are commonly used for spiritual growth.

Make sure that you try to consume these foods as raw as possible in preference of fresh to canned, baked and (last-rest) cooked. As well as losing lots of spiritual nutrients along the way, cooking brings the food farther away from nature and the alkaline properties these foods provide.

Visit this link to get a comprehensive list of foods you can include in your Psychic diet:

www.marionjaide.com/third-eye-awakening-resources/

On the other side of the dining table, here are some commonly consumed acid-forming foods that should be avoided where possible!

- Artificial sweeteners
- Alcoholic beverages
- Pastries/cakes
- Cheese, ice cream, milkshakes, yoghurt and other dairy products
- White flour
- Sugar filled juice
- Meats (chicken, mutton, fish, pork, turkey)
- Pasta
- Common salt
- Soda
- Sugar

If all these lists are too difficult for you, you can try this method for chakra healing called *eating the rainbow*.

This philosophy took birth in **Ayurveda,** the traditional medicine system in India. According to the science of Ayurveda, each color of the rainbow has a specific energy associated with the color of the chakras and the same colored foods! So to apply this principle, those with root chakra imbalances would eat tomatoes, beets, raspberries or strawberries to revive their root energies as they are all red colored fruit and vegetables.

To apply *eating the rainbow* to our third eye, we would activate our third eye energy by eating foods colored **violet** as this is the frequency associated with the third eye. For your reference here are some violet colored vegetables and fruits you can eat:

- Eggplant
- Kale
- Plums
- Purple varieties of carrot, cabbage, kohlrabi and potato

The idea is to nourish your chakras, and feel free to include the items from the list provided and give it a dash of your creativity. We encourage you to explore your options to eat these foods so you don't have to end up eating unexciting food. Some suggestions from clients to spice things up include making smoothies, shakes, salads and even teas. Check out the references section to see some great places for recipes.

Herbs

Herbs have always played a vital role in activation of chakras and sealing our connection with the energetic realms. These herbs have been found very helpful and essential in the well-being of the *Ajna* chakra.

Tulsi or Holy Basil

One of the most important, necessary and beneficial herbs in Ayurveda, this plant is very aromatic and has a wonderful flavor. This herb can totally reset your body to health and vibrancy. It contains adaptogen, which stimulates the body's non-specific resistance to harmful changes and makes it work efficiently. It derives its name from the holy texts of Hindus, is considered sacred in the land Ayurveda, India, and is commonly found.

It has the capability to help in the fulfilment of spiritual pursuits and cleansing and balancing of chakras. It has antibacterial, antiviral, antioxidant, antidepressant, diuretic and digestive properties and helps recover trauma.

You can add a teaspoon of Tulsi to your tea, it brings out a wonderfully tasty flavour, and use its stem and roots for bug and insect bites, juice for earaches and boils and you can plant it in your home. It's a tiny plant with great productivity. There are people who have had meditative experiences of ecstasy while meditating in the proximity with this plant.

Other Herbs

Some other fantastic herbs to try include:

- **Ginger:** makes our body receptive to the spirit and energy flow. It warms the body up and prepares it for higher experiences and the best part about ginger is that it goes with a variety of dishes and gels well with many other herbs.
- **Gotu Kola:** Is a companion to ginger. When our brain or body receives messages from the spirit, it contains a lot of energy and this herb helps decipher and understand those messages.
- **Wood Betony:** Clears the throat and third eye chakra and makes one more clairvoyant and clairaudient. One is more capable of manifesting the messages of the spirit within.

- **Ginkgo:** Acts like wood betony and helps activate the clairvoyant center.

- **Skullcap:** Even after you receive messages from the spirit, you may not be at ease or relaxed to differentiate between the actual messages and the messages from your ego. Skullcap helps you relax, and differentiate between the two. It strengthens the nervous system very well and works wonders even on the most irritated nerves, and helps in sleeping disorders too. It can become a member of your morning cup of spiritual tea with tulsi and ginger.

A proper diet is the foundation towards achieving healing for your third eye and extrasensory perception. With all these fruits, vegetables, herbs and combinations, you will decalcify your pineal gland in no time. Try some of these foods in your next weekly grocery shop and notice how your psychic power changes. You may just find a new culinary favourite among them too!

4

STEP TWO – PHYSICAL EXERCISE FOR PSYCHICS

In this step we will discuss an external component of third eye chakra healing: yoga and exercise.

The Third Eye chakra, also known as the 'brow chakra' which has the Pineal Gland at its base, is the seat of some of the highest spiritual faculties. Some philosophers have also opined that the Third Eye chakra is the bridge between human and cosmic elements and is responsible for generating the connection between the two.

The pineal gland which is almost the size of a pea is a dormant gland that is present in all of us. This begs the question as to how such a small gland can play such a crucial role in human existence to such an extent!

We all know that the Third Eye is also the chakra of **light**, so as with the meditations the yogic masters recommend practicing third eye exercises first thing in the morning. Yoga is fantastic first thing in the morning as it also energizes and grounds the body well for high performance throughout the day.

Many practices and yogic regimes have been used by Indian mystics since olden days and there is an exhaustive list of poses and other methods which are very helpful in activating your Third Eye chakra.

On a health note, if you are suffering from a disease or a chronic ailment, do not undertake any of the practices without consulting an expert! Play safe!

Physical Exercises

To begin with, the Third Eye chakra is the chakra of clearing the cobwebs of illusion and seeing without prejudice. There are times when we are irritated, nervous or depressed; at such times it is better not to see something and form a perception about it because our clarity of vision and perception is eclipsed and decisions or actions may go wrong. So next time, when you are angry about a bad cup of coffee, do not go on to think that your boss is a hateful man. He may not be as bad as he looks like at that moment!

Try to treat your chakra with some sound vibrations. Chant 'OM', the sacred word of yoga in a murmur and visualize the energy of sound radiate from the Third Eye and spread to your brain, eyes, etc. This vibration of sound activates your pineal gland.

Ever heard of letting your thoughts paint a picture with words? If you are in troubled state of mind and a question pops up, write it down. When you experience a peaceful state, just write down the answer as unaltered thoughts that come to your mind. If that thought in the form of an answer warms up your heart or makes it race, pursue your goal in that direction. Do not behave as if it as an emergency; be easy, warm and loving towards your decision and it'll surely work for you.

As we know that third Eye chakra denotes light, exposure to light balances and energizes this chakra. Spend some time in the warm sunlight, watch it make a water body shine or play on the leaves, your skin and hair. It helps plenty and a tan looks great!

Yogic Exercises

There is a technique known as the 'alternative nostril breathing technique'. It is a part of the complete set of breathing exercises from the yogic realm, which is known as 'Pranayama' and 'Nadi Shodhan'.

Use your finger to close your right nostril and inhale from the left nostril, steadily, not forcefully, then close the left nostril and exhale from the right one. Repeat this with the right nostril, inhale from right after blocking the left one, then release the left nostril, block the right one and exhale. Remember, steady! It balances emotions and enhances logical reasoning. You can also follow other breathing exercises from the set. There are videos and pictures available on internet and there are books too.

- Bend down on all fours with your head parallel to the ground. Hunch your back up and, breathing out, drop your head to your chest in such a way that your upper back swells up a little. Then bring your head back to the parallel position, inhaling. Repeat this with an increasing pace without straining yourself, your head will clear up and relax.
- Stand with your feet slightly apart, bend forward and try to touch the ground without bending your knees. This balances the flow of energy and channels it to the Third Eye.
- Lie down on your back, flat on the ground close to a wall. Raise your legs up with the help of the wall towards the sky and hold them straight forming a perfect 'L' shape with your body.
- Yogic asanas like gomukhasana, makarasana (crocodile pose), ardh chandrasana (half moon pose), uttana shishosana, sirsana (headstand), parsvottonasana (pyramid pose), garudasana (eagle pose), balasana (child pose), setu bandhasana (bridge pose), are some very effective exercises for the Third Eye chakra. I am not describing them here because a mere description will not make the pose perfect all the time; hence I recommend that you watch the videos on internet before practicing.

If you adopt a healthy meditative, dietary and exercise routine, you'll feel your memory, creativity, empathy and psychic power improve. All these are clear-cut signs that your discipline and hard work is paying off and your Third Eye is being energized once more.

5

STEP THREE – CRYSTALS, HERBS AND ESSENTIAL OILS

The Third Eye chakra is so important for spiritual evolution that finding ways to maintain it in a healthy state and activating it are key issues to be handled and looked after. Till we have activated this chakra, our intuition, creativity, memory, clairvoyance, and other related aspects exist in a dormant or restricted state.

What you need to do along with meditation and exercises is to take help and assistance from other sources which are available to you, like crystals, herbs and oils. There are numerous options available out there, just explore and see for yourself!

Crystals and Stones

The color of the Third Eye is Indigo, the color of wisdom, intellect and intuition. Most of the crystals and stones associated with this chakra are blue/purple/indigo in color. Like the essential oils, the crystals and stones could be used in numerous ways and they come in really pretty and luxurious options. Some of them have been elaborated upon for your convenience.

- Lapis lazuli works on all the upper three chakras and enhances their power.

- Moldavite is formed by meteorite strikes on the Earth and that is why it is considered an extra-terrestrial stone. It helps greatly in spiritual growth.

- Amethyst is very popular for the Third Eye chakra, as it can pierce through various dimensions. A perfect spiritual crystal!

- Apophyllite has huge water content and is a great medium for attaining peace and spiritual growth.

- Herkimer Diamond helps in telepathy, soul healing, higher dimensional contact, is a great healer and extremely vibrant and metaphysical.

- Indigo Kyanite pulsates with energy which greatly helps the Third Eye chakra.

Other crystals suited to third eye healing are Azurite, Emerald, Hawk's eye, Moonstone, Opal, Tanzanite, Topaz, Turquoise, Zircon, Blue Fluorite, Blue sapphire, and Purple Fluorite. And of course, diamonds work on all chakras – who would've guessed!

The best part is that these crystals/stones make great covert fashion accessories too. Wearing them as earrings is one of the best ways to send energy to the Third Eye chakra. Bracelets, pendants and even rings are useful ways to wear these crystals with style. Looking great and feeling the psychic energy, what more could you want?

Other Methods for Crystal Healing

There are many great books and resources on how to use crystals for alternative healing. Here are just some recommendations on using crystals to specifically heal the third eye:

- The Third Eye crystals can be used to massage the body

- Hold one of the Third Eye crystals in your left palm while meditating

- You can place a flat piece of crystal under your pillow when you go to bed to absorb energy while sleeping, that is when your mind has maximum relaxation.

- Placing a piece at your bed side table in order to be in its proximity is also a great way to absorb the crystals' pulsating energy.

- Place the crystals decoratively around your home or office to stay in proximity to their vibrations

Herbalism

It is important to emphasize the use of herbs again in your third eye healing beyond including them in your diet. Every herb has a different relationship with an individual. What may work for you may not work as well for your friends. **Nervines** are those herbs which work on the nerves of an individual and help soothe anger, depression, emotional upsets, etc.

Herbs are fantastic in that they can be used beyond simply eating them. Try any of the following:

- Try to obtain skin lotions, body butters and face masks that contain these herbs. Alternatively, try calling up a local herbalist to make up a body butter or cream mixture of herbs

- Make or buy a potpourri with the flowers and leaves of these herbs

- Dry and press the leaves of these herbs and display them as artworks in your home

- Get into indoor gardening and grow these herbs around the home

As well as the herbs mentioned in your psychic diet, you can try Catnip, California poppy, Chamomile, Eluethero, Flax, Ginger root, Ginkgo, Ginseng, Gotu Kola, Hops, Lavender, Lemon balm, Marshmallow, Nettle, Passion flower, Mimosa, Peppermint,

Rosemary, Sage, Skullcap, Spearmint, Spirulina, Valerian and Wood betony. These herbs all help towards activating the third eye.

These herbs are healers that work beyond the physical and psychological levels. I highly recommend you adopt these into your healing and even beauty regimes!

Essential Oils

Essential oils and its uses are one of the best ways to relax and heal. A luxurious soak in your favorite oil can really work on the physical, psychological and energy level. Just add a few drops to the bath tub, or a few drops with your massage oil, or use a diffuser to inhale and charge the room with the aroma and energy. Who knew spiritual growth could ever be so luxurious?

You can apply essential oils topically to the middle of the forehead, above the eyebrows and temples as well as using them in massage. Alternatively you can use a slow oil incense burner or scented candles to fill your body with their healing and relaxing aromas. Here are some essential oils to choose from:

Carrot seed, Galbanum, Bay laurel, Grapefruit, Myrrh, German chamomile, Nutmeg, Palo Santo, Roman chamomile, Sandalwood, Black spruce, Jasmine, Siberian fir, Silver fir, Cinnamon, Clary sage, Elemi, Frankincense, Melissa, Helichrysum, Patchouli, Rose, Vetiver, Tea tree.

- Lavender works well for all seven chakras including the *Ajna* chakra
- Rose, Neroli, Frankincense, Sandalwood and Jasmine are good for meditation
- Basil promotes growth in hair as well as healing the third eye
- Chamomile, Clary sage, Eucalyptus, Lavender, Bay, Lemon, Myrrh, Patchouli, Rosemary and Ylang-ylang can eliminate dandruff, itchy scalp and dryness too

These oils add such freshness and fragrance to hair that you may never help falling in love with them over and over again.

Additional Exercises for Third Eye Healing

If any of the above aren't to your liking, there are some short exercises and practical tips you can apply every day to heal the third eye. Firstly, as with all chakra healing and meditation, I encourage you to keep a third eye chakra journal where you will record all your psychic exposures including: dreams, visions, déjà vu experiences and voices. The truth is, your Third Eye and Pineal gland have been with you all along; you may simply need to tune in and pay attention to their higher frequency messages to receive them.

Have you ever entered a spiritual place and felt peace at how clean and decorative it is? Keep your place of meditation as clear and clean as possible to allow energy to move. Additionally, try decorating your bedroom in shades of purple or violet – the frequency of light associated with the third eye chakra – and feel the peace in your own home.

Finally, **first thing in the morning**, you can use any of the affirmations below. They have been found very effective at psychological and energy level and help tune you in to your psychic power:

- I am wise, intuitive, peaceful and connected with my inner self.
- I listen to the wisdom within me.
- I know that all is well in my world.
- I am open to bliss and grace.
- I am in tune with my divinity.
- I see and understand the "big picture".
- I am open to greater and deeper spiritual awareness.

This completes the Third Eye Awakening Step #4. Before you move on, resolve to try at least one of the techniques you've read about in this chapter. Add essential oils, crystals or herbs to your healing arsenal and feel your third eye chakra expand, spin and energize.

6

STEP FOUR – INTERNAL HEALING

In this step we will focus on the internal healing required for your third eye awakening. As your third eye is the seat of your mind, it is only appropriate that the internal focus of meditation is the best method for third eye activation. Meditating on your third eye is essential to help you experience the higher dimension and connection with the universe required for extrasensory psychic power.

What is Meditation?

For those who have not read my first book on chakra meditation, meditation is the way to find peace and connect with the spiritual universe. Meditation calms the chattering mind and lets us hear the subconscious mind, spiritual guides and the power of the universe. It is the place you go to experience the higher frequency required to access your psychic powers. For this reason, this *meditative* state is extremely helpful in progressing Third Eye healing. Meditation also helps activate the pineal gland which since childhood is normally inactive.

If you think meditating once will unblock your third eye energies, you are setting yourself up for disappointment. Like the misconceptions, illusions and calcification layers that have built up over time, nobody can reverse their third eye energies so quickly. Meditation is a continuous process and you will need to strive to meditate regularly until the third eye and your psychic powers are opened. Before you begin, you might come across difficulties in meditating at first. But do not be discouraged. Here are some tips for better meditation:

- Meditation can be perfected only by practice. Do not be impatient or give up your practice, because you can't achieve what you want right from the start.
- Be comfortable in your posture. No point trying to balance yourself in lotus position and waste time. Sit on a chair or bed.
- Take deep breaths to clam yourself, wear comfortable clothes, and keep your spine straight.
- Focus on relaxing and being simple. Do not change your practices on anybody's advice, remember everybody is different.
- Have a sacred corner or room for meditation, which is calm, clean, simple and comfortable.

Below are three third eye meditations that are helpful in activating and unblocking the third eye. Read through the steps for each meditation and choose only one to perform each day. The best time to perform third eye meditation is first thing in the morning before your physical brain fires up. As the pineal gland also responds well to light, meditating to the morning sun is the best way to reconnect with the psychic energy within. An exception to this is Meditation #2 where we meditate with our focus on the light granted to us from a flame.

As well as turning on some meditative music to enter a relaxed state, you could also try meditating to some of the powerful binaural tracks found online. Visit my website's resources page for this book for some excellent, free binaural tracks. (www.marionjaide.com/third-eye-awakening-resources/)

Meditation #1

This meditative technique is described in **Yoga**, known as a **Trataka** meditation meaning to look, or to gaze. In this meditation our focus will be internally as we gaze upon the third eye within. This is extremely good for the *Ajna* chakra activation and balancing.

1. Sit in a crossed legged or lotus mudra/position, with your spine proud and straight

2. Close your eyes and relax by taking a few deep breaths

3. Now concentrate on your pineal gland with closed eyes. To accomplish this, draw both your eyes up and allow them to meet between the eyebrows. If your eyes reach a position where they cannot come any closer and you feel that they are drawn upwards completely, then you've reached the spot.

4. Do not strain too much. You may feel extremely sensitive if you reach up to touch the point between your eyebrows where the third eye is. You'll feel a pleasant and relaxing strain, which is perfect.

5. After some time all the mind chatter will stop and any internal dialogue will become calmer. Thoughts should stop rushing.

It may take some practice to accomplish the perfection; do not lose hope. This is a very powerful technique.

Meditation #2

This meditation is a similar **Trataka** meditation, but should be performed in a dark enclosed room with the aid of candles and matches. Please remember to practice caution when dealing with fire.

1. Make your room dark and quiet.

2. Play some relaxing chant or some music which helps you

relax; this should be soft and mild.

3. Light a candle and sit in front of it, either on a chair with your feet on ground, or sit on the ground in Indian style of folded legs or the lotus position. Make sure that the candle is straight in front of your eyes and keep your spine straight.
4. Look intently (without removing your glance) at the candle. Do not strain yourself to stare. Feel the heat pulsating between your eyebrows, on the Third Eye chakra. (As it is the chakra of light).
5. For better results, chant "OM", the Vedic mantra pronounced like "AUM" with full exhalation.

This technique brings subtle but long lasting changes in the state of mind and really works at the spiritual level.

Meditation #3

Visualization is also a very effective healing process for the third eye chakra, being the source of your foresight and creativity.

To maximize the effectiveness of your *ajna* chakra meditation, bring your hands together, all fingers folded in and touching their respective counterparts on the other hand. Keep the middle fingers straight. This pose creates a resemblance to an eye - your third eye.

Tap in and unleash the energy in your *ajna* by focusing on the center point of your brow, where the third eye exists. Sometimes when we close our eyes tightly, we can feel the squeeze on our pituitary gland where the third eye chakra is. Focus your mind and energy onto this spot between your eyes. Feel the third eye chakra in its spot and see its bright indigo color.

Focus on the purple hue as you chant an "OM" or "AUM" sound. Notice how close your third eye is to your brain, where your misconceptions and illusions block your chakra from moving. Draw the psychic and mystic indigo energy around your head into the third eye chakra as you penetrate through the illusions held in your head. Fill the third eye chakra, your seat of intuition and creativity, with the indigo colored energy that is surrounding you. Continue to breathe deeply and chant.

Feel the light (or energy) from the sun/moon entering into the area and experience quicker spinning of this energy center in your head. Visualize this energy disc becoming more brightly colored and engulfing your brain and body in all shades of indigo. See the indigo light spinning clearly in your third eye as you bestow this energy into your mind's eye. Open up your intuition and creativity as your illusions melt away. You can now see clearer as your third eye chakra is released.

The Psychic's Mentality

In addition to meditation, you should aim to adopt a psychic's mindset. Here are four high frequency changes in mindset you can apply today to be in a better position to receive extrasensory perceptions.

Drop That Mind

An over-active or over-analytic mind blocks development of intuition. Be open, neutral, peaceful, and watch your intuition start taking over. Read on the practice of mindfulness, stillness and present-ness. Or practice it by going out for a walk, lying down on green grass or smelling the roses, literally, to practice being in the moment – without your brain zooming a hundred miles an hour!

Stop Competing

Peaceful and intuitive minds are not competitive. It is not necessary to be the fastest driver, the top performer, the best dressed, the best cook or even command the most psychic power! Work towards living a casual and satisfied life and your psychic development will follow.

You Are Not Alone

Psychics are able to find deeper meaning in their lives and are thus able to stop worrying over small things. Recognize that you are not the only being in the world experiencing what you are experiencing now. We are all connected by energy and we have permission to share our passions and goals with others.

Be Non-Judgemental

Everyone has intuitive thoughts and feelings all the time. The secret to developing the intuition is to be aware of those thoughts without judging. Try to keep yourself neutral and peaceful so that you can understand and embrace intuition when it comes. It may be a key to a deeper aspect of your life that you've been looking for.

Try any of the three meditation methods above to connect to the Universe, open your third eye chakra and experience the psychic power it provides. When it comes to any chakra healing, always remember that internal healing is just as important as external treatments. Like all spiritual healing, patience and regularity are the keys to success!

7

STEP FIVE – MONITOR YOUR PSYCHIC PROGRESS

While we measure work with time and money, and exercise with bathroom scales, what measures can we use to monitor our psychic and third eye power? In this last step, we will examine the signs of psychic experience, and ways to soothe ourselves before feeling overwhelmed.

Your very first psychic encounter at the start of this journey may be overwhelming. But fear not, this is only because your third eye has been dormant since puberty. Like any muscle under stress for the first time, the pineal gland needs gradual exposure to psychic energy before its full power is realized.

Sensitivity to energies

When your Third Eye chakra starts being activated, you become sensitive to all kinds of energies. If you interact with people with negative energies or are in a negative environment, it may disturb your own energy and make you feel panicked or erratic. On the positive side, this is a sign of third eye progress; however you also have to be careful about the kind of exposure you have and the company you keep in this state.

One such way is to try bathing in lukewarm water, i.e. not cold nor hot. Visualize that with the flow of water all the negativity that you have gathered is getting washed away from your body, mind and soul. This is very helpful in cleansing the negative energy.

Another technique is that when you are with such people, visualize that a golden protective light has encased you and negativity cannot touch you. This builds a protective layer, you are fortified and you can keep your own energy intact and vibrant.

Increased sense of perception

You may also start to be extremely aware of things that aren't in others' experience. For example, you may go to sleep and still be aware of everything happening around you. Another way this may manifest is if you are able to sense the energies or auras of people around you. Congratulations, these are all signs of an opening third eye!

This feeling at times can sometimes make people restless or oversensitive. A strategy to continue these perceptions but also feel at ease is to work on your other chakras, in particular your Solar Plexus and Root chakras. These will help you feel more at home in your own body, regardless of the extrasensory influences from your psychic eye. Once you learn to accept your psychic perceptions, you will experience the joy of this great state – fully relaxed and fully aware!

Dreams, Visions and Projections

Another sign of third eye healing is awareness or increased frequency of the following phenomena:

- **Projection** or **Astral Projection**. The sensation of an out of body experience, usually occurring while sleeping.
- **Lucid Dreams**. Being conscious that you are dreaming or even consciously affecting your dreams. Many psychics aim to open their third eye to benefit from lucid dreaming.

- **Déjà Vu.** Ever saw something and feel like you've experienced the same thing more than once? Some believe the experience of déjà vu is simply memories of your astral body. Either way, increasing frequency of déjà vu indicates your third eye is opening.

Keep a diary or journal to record all your third eye experiences. You may find over time your awareness increasing; this is fantastic news and means your third eye healing is progressing!

Dangers of Opening the Third Eye

Have you heard the phrase that **"Everything comes at a price"**?

Opening or activation of the Third Eye also has its issues and it's better to know them before you get into it. Opening of the Third Eye has a symbolism indicating that it is a way to open your perception and have access to higher dimensions. It allows you to see this entire universe as a whole. The Third Eye finds maximum reference, reverence, importance and analysis in Hinduism. Different cultures have different ways of working on the Third Eye. The benefits of working on it are many but you should also know what 'negative' things you may experience.

Over-energized Third Eyes

Some third eye healers have reported increased headaches and physical vibrations felt throughout their body. If you feel these too, you may well have opened your third eye before you are ready. Headaches and over-sensitivity are the first indicators of opening the third eye before you are ready. As well as the physical discomfort, your mind may be racing too fast making you feel anxious or unsure.

Visions and Hallucinations

You may see images, colors or visions that will not make any sense at all. Or even worse, your mind interprets these things as spirits, ghosts or demons. For example, if you go to sleep, suddenly you start seeing things that may appear to be demonic or paranormal. It may confuse you, make you feel fearful or space you out as nothing appears logical.

Some images and visions you see may appear to be blurred too. If they are blurred it means that your chakra is still weak and your access to other dimensions is not complete. Also, do not be afraid if the visions just flash or go by too fast. Your third eye is growing and it takes time to reach stability.

Disturbed Spirits

You may also have access to dimensions which are somewhat low, i.e., disturbed spirits are found there. Spirits of murderers and people who committed suicides or rapes and have not been forgiven are very disturbed and if you connect to them, you are bound to feel disturbed too.

You may also start to hear voices in your head that you may not normally hear. The things you hear can be interpreted to be dark or even scary.

The Solution: Chakra Self-Defence

All of these experiences are signs of third eye awakening. However, the fact that you fear them or you feel negative after these experiences is a sign that you may not be ready for those frequencies.

Do not feel discouraged if you receive a negative vision. They are merely signs that your physical presence is not comfortable in its own skin. These things may look scary, but the only reason you interpret their gestalt as fear is because your body is interpreting them as so. You must ask yourself, what is there to be fearful about in the spiritual realm? We have been trained and indoctrinated to think spirits and ghosts can harm us, but with strong chakras and positive auras, it is possible to stay firm in our bodies and observe these psychic energies without judgment.

In order to feel at ease, you will have to improve your vibrations to feel neutral about any observations. Instead of trying to force your third eye open, I encourage you to work on your other chakras for a while to help build a strong aura. Only once you feel comfortable with yourself and are less fearful of what you may face should you resume your third eye healing.

Some other warnings and tips to open the third eye chakra include:

- Drugs and other stimulants do not help chakra opening and there are no genuine drugs to attain this purpose.
- Do not continue if you are not ready for it. Make sure that you are not feeling fearful or confused.
- If you are stuck, find a reliable practitioner and trust only an expert.

If you want some more detail, refer to the additional resources at the end of this book. As well as these resources, there are some organizations that have mastery over these things and know their job well. You can check them out: Yogada Satsanga Society of India by Paramhansa Yogananda, Isha Foundation by Sadhguru Jaggi Vasudev, and Art of Living by Sri Sri Ravishankar are truly genuine organizations.

In this step we discussed the final lesson: knowing and understanding what happens when your Third Eye is truly open. Beginning to access psychic power for the first time in years can be a frightful experience to those without the knowledge to deal with it. Do not be discouraged or embarrassed if you do not experience immediate results. Third Eye awakening is not a race, and activation most definitely should not be rushed. The best things in life take time. With patience and persistence you will see and feel real, life-lasting psychic results.

8

CONCLUSION

Anyone can unlock their psychic powers by following the five *Third Eye Activation steps* in this book. Eating an alkaline diet combined with the power of yoga, exercise and alternative healing is the best way to bring you toward an awakened Third Eye. But of course, the critical part of the healing process – focused meditation – will be where most of your chakra and Third Eye balancing occurs! Remember to meditate frequently in your journey and monitor your psychic progress as you heal.

The psychic and mental power granted by the Third Eye chakra lets people lead extraordinary lives. In the physical world, improved cognition, creativity and intuition can bring business and personal success. I mean, wouldn't it be great to trust and follow your intuitions even though the future is always in motion? In the higher spiritual frequencies, an open Third Eye chakra is also a necessary step towards attaining complete chakra balance, a radiant aura and greater connection to and peace with the Universe – a lengthy, yet highly rewarding pursuit.

Once you experience your psychic power through the Third Eye, I encourage you to seek healing for your other Chakras and indeed open your mind to other spiritual concepts. After all, spiritual healing is a process that takes many days, weeks, months and even lifetimes.

We are all spiritual and vibrational beings, seeking the best for our existence. There are no prerequisites to living a free and happy life.

And there are no requirements to access your psychic power - except for your will to begin. With the knowledge in this book, you *can* start your Third Eye awakening and claim your psychic power today!

ADDITIONAL RESOURCES

If you are interested in further reading, please consider these additional resources.

Other Books

Some very interesting and informative books have been written about the chakras. They are of great help and really work as a guide to people looking for spiritual growth. They will give you an insight and understanding about the spiritual journey and the related aspects. Here are some for names for your help:

- **Diary of a psychic** by Sonia Choquette, it guides and aids in the journey towards being psychic.
- **Awakening the Third Eye** by Britannica Creations is of help in reference to the Third Eye chakra.
- **Third Eye Chakra** by Viv Rosser is a part of the entire set of seven books on each chakra

Alkaline Diet Recipes

Here are some web links to find some delicious psychic's recipes:

- http://www.earthenergyhealings.com
- http://www.about.com.holistichealing

Don't forget to keep up with Marion Jaide's blog and resources section for this book at www.marionjaide.com

AUTHOR'S NOTE

Thank you for reading my book, *Third Eye Awakening in 5 Easy Steps*. If you found my book useful in your third eye awakening, please let myself and other readers know by reviewing it in Amazon.

In invite you to visit my author website at www.marionjaide.com to say hello and get the free e-newsletter for news on my up-coming books.

Lastly, if you have any tips, advice or feel I've missed something important, please email me at marion@marionjaide.com – I appreciate your feedback

All the best,
Marion Jaide

Printed in Great Britain
by Amazon.co.uk, Ltd.,
Marston Gate.